THE VERY LOWLY

The Very Lowly

 A Meditation on Francis of Assisi

CHRISTIAN BOBIN

Translated by MICHAEL H. KOHN

New Seeds

BOSTON & LONDON   2006

New Seeds Books
An imprint of Shambhala Publications, Inc.
Horticultural Hall
300 Massachusetts Avenue
Boston, Massachusetts 02115
www.newseeds-books.com

9 8 7 6 5 4 3 2 1

First New Seeds Edition
Printed in the United States of America

Designed by Ann Twombly

♾ This edition is printed on acid-free paper that meets the
American National Standards Institute z39.48 Standard.
Distributed in the United States by Random House, Inc.,
and in Canada by Random House of Canada Ltd

Library of Congress Cataloging-in-Publication Data
Bobin, Christian.
[Très-bas. English]
The very lowly: A meditation on Francis of Assisi/by Christian Bobin;
translated by Michael H. Kohn.—1st New Seeds ed.
Originally published: The secret of Francis of Assisi. Boston, Mass.:
Shambhala; New York: Distributed in the U.S. by Random House, 1997.
ISBN-13 978-1-59030-310-8
ISBN-10 1-59030-310-5
1. Francis, of Assisi, Saint, 1182–1226—Meditations. I. Title.
BX4700.F6B5413   2006
271'.302—dc22   2005052215
[B]

To Ghislaine Marion,
who liberates with her laughter
all the roads of ink

Contents

THE VERY LOWLY

A Question
That Despairs
of an Answer

"THE CHILD LEFT WITH THE ANGEL and the dog followed behind."* This sentence is in the Bible. It is a sentence from the Book of Tobit in the Bible. The Bible is a book composed of many books, and in each one of them are many sentences, and in each one of these sentences, many stars, olive trees, and fountains, little asses and fig trees, grain fields and fish—and the wind, everywhere the wind, the mauve of the evening wind, the pink of the morning breeze, the black of the great storms. Today's books are made of paper. Yesterday's books were made of skin. The Bible is the only book made of air. It is a flood of ink and wind, a mad book, adrift in its meaning, as lost in its pages as the wind on supermarket parking lots, in women's hair,

*Tobit 6:1 New English Bible.

1

in the eyes of children. A book that is impossible to hold calmly between our hands for a prudent, distant reading. It takes flight on the spot, scatters the sand of its phrases through our fingers. We take the wind in our hands and very quickly we stop. As at the beginning of a love affair, we say: I'll stop here, I've found everything, I'll stop here with the first smile, the first meeting, the first chance phrase. "The child left with the angel, and the dog followed behind." This sentence suits Francis of Assisi marvelously well. We know little of him, and that is for the best. What we know about people keeps us from knowing them. What we say about them, imagining that we know what we are saying, makes it difficult to see them. We say, for example, "Saint Francis of Assisi." We say it like someone sleepwalking, without coming out of the sleep of language. We do not say it, we let it say itself. We let the words come out. They come out in an order that is not our own, which is the order of a lie, of death, of life in society. Very few genuine words are exchanged in a day, really very few. Perhaps we only fall in love in order finally to begin to speak. Perhaps we only open a book in order finally to begin to hear. "The child left with the angel, and the dog followed behind." In this sentence you see neither the angel nor the child. You only see the dog; you sense its joyful mood, you watch it follow the two invisible ones: the child made invisible by its carefreeness, the angel made invisible by his simplicity. The dog, yes, we see it. Behind. Lagging. It follows the other two. It follows their trail and sometimes gets involved in little amusements of its own; it wanders into a field, freezes at the sight of a moor hen or a fox. Then in two bounds it links up again with the child and the angel. Roving, playful. The child and the angel are together on the same track. Maybe the child has the angel by the hand, guiding him so that the angel, who moves in the visible world like a blind man in broad daylight, will not be too troubled. The child hums, says whatever comes into its head, the angel smiles and goes along with it—and the dog is still there behind those two, sometimes on the right, sometimes on the left. This dog is in the Bible. There are whales, lambs, birds, and serpents, but very few dogs. In fact you know of no other dog but that one, roaming the roads, following its two masters: laughter and silence, playfulness and grace. The dog Francis of Assisi.

It is a question that does not find an answer. It is a question that despairs of an answer. It bangs itself like a fly banging against a pane of glass until it finds the open air of an answer. It is a childish question. It is asked by a soul tossing and turning in a fistful of blue sky, in a silence that is too big for it: where do I come from, I who was not always here? Where was I when I hadn't been born? Today we have the shortest possible answer: you come from the copulation of your father and mother. You are the fruit of a few sighs and a little bit of pleasure. Moreover, those sighs and that pleasure are not indispensable— nowadays we need only a test tube. The most up-to-date answer is, you come from a spermatozoon and an ovum. There is no question of anything before that. There is no more a before than there is a beyond. You are nothing more than a twitch of matter with itself, a roundabout road that nothingness takes, only to rejoin itself at the end. In the thirteenth century, the century of Francis of Assisi, the answer was longer, much longer, though it turned out to be no more capable of doing away with the question. In the thirteenth century a person came from God and returned to Him. The answer in its entirety was to be found in the Bible; the Book and the answer were one

4

and the same. It was an answer thousands of pages long. It was not so much in the Bible as in the heart of the person who read the Bible in order to find the answer. And he could not really read without making his reading enter into his every day. The answer was not read but felt. It was not a professor's answer. Professors are people who teach others the words they themselves have found in books. But we do not learn from words in a book made of air. We receive its freshness, a little at a time. We are startled by the breath of an utterance: I loved you well before you were born. I will love you well after the end of time. I love you in all the eternities. Before he fell into a dazed slumber in his mother's belly, Francis of Assisi bathed in this utterance. It was kept closed up in the Bible like gold at the bottom of a coffer. It was let out for holidays, it was let out in the gestures of work and in the gestures of repose. It pervaded the curves of the land, the breath of beasts in barns, the taste of heavy bread. And before this utterance was in the Bible, where was it, where did it come from? It hovered over the voidness of the lands and over the voidness of hearts, it prowled with the wind in the deserts. It was first. It was always there. The word of love is before everything, even before love. In the beginning there was only that: the voice without words, the breath of gold enveloping God, Francis of Assisi, and Tobias's dog, pressed together, their breathing blended.

I loved you. I love you. I will love you. Flesh is not all that is necessary for being born. This utterance, this word, is also necessary. It comes from far away. It comes from the blue distance of the heavens, it sinks into living beings, it flows under the flesh of a living thing like a subterranean stream of pure love. It is not necessary to know the Bible to hear it. It is not necessary to believe in God to be brought to life by His breath. Every page of the Bible is impregnated with this utterance, but the leaves of trees, the coats of animals, and every mote of dust floating in the air are also impregnated with it. The subtle fundament of matter, its final kernel, its ultimate point, is not matter but this utterance. I love you. I love you with an eternal love, eternally directed toward you—dust mote, animal, human being. Before hovering over cradles, before dancing on the lips of mothers, this utterance finds its way through the voices that create an era, that give it its tone and its color. Words of war and of commerce. Words of glory and disaster. Words of the deaf. From the side, from below, from above, the spirit of the wind, that mad resonance, the humming in the red blood: I love you. Well before you were born. Well after the end of time. I love you in all the eternities. Francis of Assisi comes from that. He comes from that and he returns to it, as one returns to bed deep in the arms of a beautiful woman.

But let's get a little bit closer. Let's listen to the sounds of the world at the window. The sound of gold, the sound of the sword, the sound of prayers. People counting their pennies behind heavy drapes. People brewing black wine in the depths of their castles. People muttering beneath the angels' lace. The merchant, the warrior, and the priest—these three share the thirteenth century. And then there is another class. It is in the shadows, too pulled back into itself for any light to find it. It is like the prime matter of the other three. The merchants draw the manual labor they require from it. The warriors find what they need to renew their armies in it. The priests sniff out in it the souls that are to their taste. Those three expect something as a reward for their work: fortune, glory, or salvation. This class does not expect anything, not even the passage of time, the numbing of pain. This is the class of the poor. It is of the thirteenth century and it is of the twentieth century. It is of all the centuries. It is as old as God, as mute as God, as lost in ancientness and silence as He is. It will give Francis of Assisi his true face. A face much more beautiful than the painted wooden ones in churches, much purer than the ones by great painters. A simple face of a poor man. A poor face of a poor man, an idiot, a beggar.

The autumn of 1182 in Italy. A sentence coming from the depths of the centuries turns in the air, floats for a moment above a house in the town of Assisi, then melts into a newborn baby asleep in its cradle. There is no sound. No change in appearances. No one gets upset. No one sees anything. The child does not wake up. Great things always begin with sleep. Great things always begin by the thinnest edge. There are few events in a lifetime. Wars, celebrations, and all those things that create a stir are not events. An event is the life that transpires in a lifetime. An event has the form of a cradle. It has a cradle's weakness and ordinariness. An event is a cradle of life. We never witness its arrival. We are never contemporaries of the invisible. It is not until after the fact, only a long time after, that we guess something must have happened.

The child and the angel departed from Assisi without anyone noticing them. A dog followed them, three steps behind.

In its sleep, the newborn baby gave a sigh.

Moreover,
There Is No Such Thing
as a Saint

SHE IS BEAUTIFUL. NO, SHE IS MORE than beautiful. She is life itself in its most tender, auroral brilliance. You do not know her. You have never seen a single portrait of her, but the evidence is there, the evidence of her beauty—the light on her shoulders when she leans over the cradle, when she gets up to listen to the breathing of little Francis of Assisi, who is not called Francis yet, who is no more than a wee lump of pink and wizened flesh, a human infant, more helpless than a kitten or a shrub. She is beautiful because of the love she strips from herself in order to cover the nakedness of the child. She is beautiful in virtue of the weariness she rises above each time she has to go to the child's room. All mothers have this beauty. All of them have this soundness, this truth, this sanctity. All mothers have this grace, which is such as to rouse jealousy in

God Himself, the Solitary One beneath His tree of eternity. Yes, you cannot imagine her other than covered in this robe of her love. A mother's beauty infinitely surpasses the glory of nature. It is an unimaginable beauty, the only one that you can imagine for this woman attending to the stirrings of her infant. Christ never speaks of beauty. It is the only company he keeps, but under its true name: love. Beauty comes from love as daylight comes from the sun, as the sun comes from God, as God comes from a woman exhausted from childbirth. Fathers go to war, to the office, sign contracts. Fathers are in charge of society. That is their business, their great affair. A father is someone who represents something other than himself in the relationship to his child, and who believes in what he represents: law, reason, experience. Society. A mother does not represent anything in the relationship to her child. She does not stand in relationship to it, but is around it, inside, outside, everywhere. She raises the child up at arm's length and presents it to eternal life. Mothers are in charge of God. That is their passion, their sole occupation, their loss and their empowerment at the same time. To be a father is to play the role of a father. To be a mother is an absolute mystery, a mystery without reference point, an absolute that is not relative to anything, an impossible task that is nevertheless fulfilled, even by bad mothers. Even bad mothers stand in this nearness to the absolute, this intimacy with God that fathers will never know, diverted as they are by their desire to fill their post, to stand firm in their rank. Mothers have no rank, no post. They are born at the same time as their children. They do not have, as fathers do, a head start on the child—the head start of experience, of a comedy acted out time and again in society. Mothers grow up in life at the same time as their child, and as the child is the equal of God from the time of its birth, from the beginning mothers are inside the holy of holies, fulfilled by everything, ignorant of everything that fulfills them. And if all pure beauty comes from love, where does love come from? From what matter does its matter derive, from what nature its supernaturalness? Beauty comes from love. Love comes from attention. Simple attention to the simple; humble attention to humble things; living attention to all lives, and surely to that of the little cub in its cradle, incapable of feeding itself, incapable of everything but tears. The first knowledge of the newborn, the single possession of the prince of the crib, is his gift of complaint, his claim on the love far away, his screams in the direction of a life too distant—and it is the mother who gets up and responds. It is God who wakes up and arrives, responding every time, every time attentive above and beyond weariness. The weariness of the first days of the world, the weariness of the first years of childhood. Everything comes from that. Apart from that, there is nothing. There is no greater holiness than that of mothers exhausted by the diapers to be washed, the formula to be heated, the bath to be given. Men hold the world. Mothers hold the eternal element that holds the world and men. The future holiness of little Francis of Assisi, for the moment besmirched with milk and tears, will only reach its fullness through imitation of this maternal treasure—through sharing out, to beasts, to trees, and to everything alive, what mothers have always contrived for the benefit of the newborn. Moreover, there is no such thing as a saint. There is only holiness. Holiness is joy. It is the foundation of everything. Motherhood is that which sustains the foundation of everything. Motherhood is weariness overcome, the death swallowed back without which no joy would come. To say of someone that he is a saint is only to say that he has revealed himself through his life as a wonderful con-

ductor of joy, as we say of a metal that it is a good
conductor when it lets heat pass without loss, or
almost; or as we say of a mother that she is a good
mother when she lets weariness consume her to the
last drop, or almost.

Pietro di Bernardone—that was the name of his
father. A cloth merchant. The father was already in
business. The son inherited his fortune and his taste
for finery. Lady Pica was the name of his mother. She
was not from Assisi; she was from far away. She lived
in Provence. The father went there on a business trip
and came back with all the gold in the world in his
arms: the love of this beautiful woman, his finest
business deal without a doubt, the finest fabric he
ever held between his fingers. The mother was a
stroke of genius for the father. From time immemorial, men have traveled great distances, left their
country and their childhood behind, in order to find
a wife. Even if they marry a neighbor, it is in the
darkest corner of themselves that they look for her
and find her. For a man, a woman is the thing
farthest away in the world. But there is something
still farther away than far away; there is something still darker than a man's heart. The father went
off to find the mother in a faraway place, the courts

of Provence, in the darkness of the songs of nightin-
gales and troubadours. The twelfth century in Provence was blessed by the angels. They descended
incognito, taking advantage of their Master's having
fallen asleep. There they invented a way of loving that
had never existed before, that has never brightened
the world again since: courtly love. In it, a man lets
go of his weapons and pride in exchange for the
weakness of a song. If he competes with others, it is
only in beauty, not in strength. As for the woman, she
is for the most part another man's wife, the wife of a
lord or a king. By causing her name to shine everywhere on earth, the lover widens the distance that
separates him from his lady, until this distance con-
tains the entire world like a fish at the bottom of a
net. Everything—nature, body, and soul—comes to
find its place under the sun of this one lady. The
space that separates him from her is filled with her
laughter. It is a sacred space. Song opens it up, the
voice can fly in it. It is a happy distance. Love fills it
without ever obliterating it. *Fin amor,* love from afar.
It is a strange kind of love. In it, earth is like a piece of
heaven. In it, body and soul fuse in the lilt of a voice.
This lasted until the middle of the thirteenth century.
This music finally dragged God from His slumbers.

He stepped in and put things back in order. The last of the songs no longer rose to the bedchamber of the lady of the manor but fell back as snow onto the hands of the Virgin Mary. The letter of love remained the same—the same words, the same madness in the singing. Only the address had changed. The addressee was suddenly farther away than the young ladies of Provence. Just a little bit farther. Such was heaven in Provence of the twelfth century, crackling with voices, saturated with trills and words of love. Such was the heaven that surrounded, like the blue in a painting, the face of Lady Pica when her businessman husband discovered her. Not that Pietro di Bernardone had the soul of a troubadour. In business there is no time for the eternal. There is little occasion to care about what is far away. One proceeds a step at a time, from the money harvested today to the money planted for tomorrow. But it is not a matter of indifference that Francis of Assisi had for a mother one of these girls grown under the heavens of Provence. Mothers nurture their little ones with milk and with dreams. Their milk comes up from the deep parts of the flesh. It comes out of the breast as out of a happy wound. Mothers' dreams come up from the most secret part of their childhood. They come to

17

their lips in lullabies, they envelop the newborn child in an infinitely penetrating sweetness, like a perfume that never goes stale even over many years. No, it is not a matter of indifference that the mother of Francis of Assisi came from Provence, from that earth where men abandoned the health of a warrior for the fever of a song.

At first the child was called John. It was the mother's choice. He was baptized with this name in the absence of his father, who had gone to France again on business. On his return the father got rid of the name like someone picking a weed. He covered it up with another name: Francis.

Two names, one on top of the other. Two lives, one under the other. The first name comes right out of the Bible. It opens the New Testament and closes it. John the Baptist proclaimed the coming of Christ, took river water in the hollow of his hands to give a pretaste of a crazy freshness, of a rain shower of insane love. John the Evangelist wrote down what happened and how what is past remains in passing. John of the waters and John of the inks. The mother wanted this first name. What a mother wants for a first name she slips between the body and soul of the child, well buried like a lavender sachet between two sheets. John of the water hands, John of the golden mouth. And on top of that is the other first name, the other life. Francis of France, heart of air, blood of Provence. Through his family name a child is connected to the heap of his parents' dead forebears. Through his first name he is connected with the fertile immensity of the living, the whole field of the possible: to praise strong love like an evangelist or caress weak life like a troubadour. And why not do both things, be them both?—the evangelist and the troubadour, the apostle and the lover.

The Sweetness of Nothingness

AND THE CHILD GREW UP. HE GREW up as children do, like a tree plunging the roots of its arms into the maternal earth, drawing its nourishment from the undergrowth of speech, multiplying its tendrils, raising the branches of its thoughts into the light of the outside. Childhood is what nourishes life. What nourishes childhood? The parents and the family circle, for one part. Places, the magic of places, for another part. And God, for the rest, which is nearly all of it. Less the God of the Bible—the gardener God, the builder—than the God who fails to foresee the rains of summer and one's first sorrows, God the poacher of passing time. A God like a slightly crazy mother, a God like a mother who gives a caress and a slap in a single gesture. That God is the first one we encounter in life, before the other one, well before the other one. It is the same one but in a more real form, much closer. It is possible to negotiate with the God of the Bible. You can make deals with Him, have meetings, adjourn and resume. You can even struggle with Him, taking a chance on His weakness. But with God the nurturer of childhood, there is not a thing you can do. He is the part of childhood that is beyond control, the unplanned part of education—which is the part of the infinite. There is no believing in Him. Believing is giving your heart. This God of the simple hours has already taken the heart of the child in the cradle. He plays with it according to His whim. It is a difficult thing to understand, in the twentieth century as in the thirteenth century. In the thirteenth century because a shadow was made out of it; in the present, too much power, then too much nothingness. Little children of the twentieth century, your parents are tired. They no longer believe in anything. They ask you to carry them on your shoulders, to give them heart and strength. Little children of modern times, you are kings in the desert. Little children of the thirteenth century, not much importance is placed on you. You are like a flock sometimes seized by fever, scattered by wars, famine, or the plague. You are not spoken to very often in your first years. You hardly get looked at, and then with that tender look that is given to the farm dogs you play with in the dust of the yards. Little savages of the thirteenth century, you grow up unnoticed under the eyes of everyone, mixed up with the hostlers in the stables and the chickens in the big hall. Who saw the child Francis grow up? Apart from God, almost nobody. Not his father, too taken up with his journeys, his money, and his cloth. His mother, a little. The genius of motherhood has its eclipses. There is the mother who watches over the child she loves without preventing it from going its own way. There is the mother who torments herself for the child she loves by trying to change its course. There are Martha and Mary, the two sisters encountered by the passing Christ. Martha was concerned about order and food, awhirl in her kitchen, lost in the sound of dishes and boiling water. Mary, her apron rolled up under a bench—Mary sitting on the ground, her legs folded under her like the wings of a bird in a moment of repose, face open, hands empty—Mary was concerned about the love without which all order is sad, all food dull. Martha and Mary. The scattered one and the collected one. The unresting one and the pacified one. Mothers are both, often at the same time. A mother's caring for

23

her child blinds her as much as it illuminates her. She sees the flesh of her flesh. She sees the child living, she never sees him growing up. She sees the child in the eternity of his age, she never sees the passage from one age to another, from one eternity to the following one. One day she turns around and looks with astonishment upon this strapping youth who has just walked into the house, this man self-consciously aware of his own strength, and she no longer understands how so much force and so much awkwardness could have come out of her. For though her child may have grown up, her own heart has not aged but is still burning within her as with the first pains of childbirth. . . .

What do the texts say about Francis's childhood? Nothing. They don't say anything. They rush right to his adolescence as to the real beginning of everything. Forty years after Francis's death Jacques de Voragine, a Dominican, the future archbishop of Genoa, wrote *The Golden Legend*, a collection of the lives of the saints. This book resembles nothing more than a child's drawing. A child's drawing goes right to the essential. If life feels blocked, the child draws a house with no door. If life is lilting along, he puts in lots of windows, flowers, suns. The same is true of the miniatures of the Middle Ages, where the dress of the great lady is bigger than her castle, where a horse's eye rivals the oval of the moon. It is not that we are dealing here with some sort of juvenile stage in art or a childish incapacity of the hand. Rather, the painter is expressing a perspective different from reason's indifferent geometrical one. He is following the perspective of the heart, which depicts what is not, so that what is can be seen better. An example. You are waiting for someone. You are waiting for your lover. She is going to come. She said so. She promised. She is going to come along this stretch of road. You stare at the horizon, you look at the landscape (what is she doing, she should already be here). In the landscape there are things (a forest, houses, a road) of various sizes. When she finally arrives, all the proportions of the landscape are suddenly out of whack. The diminutive silhouette at the end of the road immediately appears as large as the forest, the houses, or the road. She who, in the eyes of the geometrician, would be no more than a speck in the distance, in the eye of the lover becomes bigger than the universe. We see according to the dimensions of his hope. The thirteenth century has a heart full of hope, which gives the faces of the Romanesque churches eyes that are so big, eyes that are so round. Jacques de Voragine wrote his book the way a child draws, dipping his fingers in the ink and tracing some simple figures on the page. *The Golden Legend* is a collection of saints caught in the midflight of a word or a gesture. As many saints as there are ways of fluttering like a butterfly in the light. Saints with wings rich like velvet, saints with dragonfly wings, saints with long antennae, saints with fine insect feet. And nothing, ever, about childhood. As though childhood had no role to play in the grace of taking flight. As though butterflies did not come from caterpillars. For Francis of Assisi, there is just a pen stroke, a wrinkle in the paper: "Francis, the servant and friend of the Most High, lived in vanity until the age of nearly twenty years." This was said by a man of the Church. For this kind of man, vanity means nothingness. The chirping of the first words: vanity, nothingness. The fragile dance of the first steps: vanity, nothingness. The wonder at the first snowflakes, at the profound softness of summer evenings; the mad laughter and the tears in the eyes, the sores on the knees and the carefreeness in the soul: vanity. Nothingness. Jacques de Voragine was a man of his time, for which childhood was a passing disease. If any heed at all was paid to it, it was to see in it nothing but a mortifying testimony to human weakness. The child is to the adult what the flower is to the fruit. Many a winter might cut off the passage of one to the other, many a storm. The child at this time is at the lowest point in creation, not far from madmen or animals. The only complete reception it gets is in the word of Christ. Jacques de Voragine was a theologian. He comments on this word, and the ruckus he makes with his commentaries prevents him from hearing it. He is an organization man, and he names his God following the model of the military hierarchy of the clergy: the Most High. This is forgetting about the impatience of Christ, who pushed aside his sensible apostles to make room for children. This is forgetting that nothing can be known about the Most High except through the Most Low, through this God the height of childhood, this God on the ground level of one's first falls, with one's nose in the grass.

The thirteenth century is a century of builders. Next to the stone churches a church of words is erected, the *Summa* of Saint Thomas Aquinas. Hundreds of thoughts depend for their support on this keystone: "Grace does not destroy nature, it perfects it." We must content ourselves with this sentence for our vision of the child of Assisi. It will enable us to catch a glimpse into those obscure years if we write it like this: sainthood does not destroy childhood, it perfects it. As for the rest, for further details, in looking at the adult one discovers the child. The growth of the spirit is the inverse of the growth of the flesh. The body grows by taking on size. The spirit grows by losing height, by losing hauteur. Sainthood reverses the laws of maturity: the man is the flower, childhood is the fruit.

Francis, the servant and friend of the Most Low, lived in sweetness until the age of nearly twenty years.

The Unicorn,
the Salamander,
and the Cricket

HE IS NOW HIS FATHER'S HEIGHT. HE goes behind the counter and helps with sales. He is now a boy with a talent for business. He has thirty-six hands for unfolding the cloth, ten thousand words for praising the manufacture of a piece of silk. Not a better salesman in the country than the eldest son of Bernardone, as any customer will tell you—especially the female clients. A good-looking lad with bright eyes, broad shoulders, and the white hands of a girl. People ask to see pieces of cloth they don't need, they pause over fabrics they will never buy, just for the pleasure of listening to him and eating him up with their eyes. And in the end they leave with the pieces of cloth, they leave with the fabrics.

Twenty years and some dust. The twenty years are the body's, the dust is the soul's. He thinks little about his soul. He lets it flutter about in his heart, makes a place for it beside his friends, beside the pretty women of Assisi, beside the wine, the gambling, and the singing. It is a very small, dusty place. A room in the heart, the most remote, the least frequented. He goes into it for a few hours during the year, at Christmastime, at Easter. And that is enough. He believes in it, of course, but as in other invisible things—unicorns, for example. For him, the existence of the soul is neither more nor less a fable than that of the unicorn. It requires no more care. The soul is part of the bird family. Before he joins this family, Francis belongs to the family of unicorns, described as follows in a medieval bestiary: "It takes such pleasure in the scent of virgins and virginity that when hunters want to catch one, they put a young virgin on its path. When it sees her, the unicorn goes to her and falls asleep on her bosom, and there it is—he is caught." But the hunter had not been born who could catch handsome Francis. Though he may have wooed many a woman, he did not fall asleep with any of them. Twenty-year-old arms are made for the waists of young women, it is true. But twenty-year-old legs are made to walk to the ends of the earth. At the top of the legs there is a sun, a force. The body is a planet that revolves around this sun in perpetual motion. Priests are sure to remind you on Sunday that you have a soul. From the height of their flesh, they let fly at your skull with words hard as stones. We listen to them with our eyes lowered, crammed in our pew, pitiful. We let the storm pass. Then we quickly get back to the essential: the young women chatting on their way out of the mass, fresh as angels. Contemplating them is a delight. A delight and a torment. Now beauty, there is a real mystery, one much more interesting than that of the soul. The beauty of a young woman's face is there before you like perfection, but it is not a perfection that closes back in on itself, but perfection that calls out, that makes a promise—and fails to keep it. The hand of God is behind it. The hand of God or the hand of the devil, you don't know which. And at twenty you couldn't care less. You are sure of only one thing: the body is eternal, much more so than the soul. There is no need for proof—at twenty, you just feel it. Furthermore, this is in fact half of the truth that priests give out, though without any real conviction: they talk to us about the resurrection of the body and the soul, do they not? That means the body is eternal too—especially the body. So you have half the truth, and with any part of the truth you can

31

already see clearly in the world, you can already see fairly far into your life. For the rest, there is time. And you have something better than time: you are twenty years old—to say nothing of the dust.

The money that comes in at the store he spends on gambling. The love that comes into his heart he spends at parties. What he has, what he is, he burns. He has something of the unicorn in him, and then something of the salamander too: "The salamander lives on fire alone. A cloth is made from his skin that no flame can burn." The scion of the Bernardone family is cloaked in such a cloth, which is beyond price. Friends come and go. Young women come and go. The money comes and goes. His mother sighs and then smiles. His father grumbles and then shuts up.

When he is asked about his future, Francis replies: "Don't you know that miracles await me, that I'll be a great knight, that I'll marry a princess who'll give me lots of children?" In this reply you can sense the mother's smile, the madness of a love passed from the heart of the mother to the heart of the son, like a precious wine poured from one glass into another without losing any of its sparkle. But there is more than a mother's fever in these words of her son. There is also God's smile present in this naive self-affirmation, in this childish lust for life. The sweetness of life, the love of oneself: in these the Most Low is present incognito, His mocking presence unperceived by the moralists who look for Him in thunderbolts from heaven or in the crypts of acts of penance. The love of self is to the love of God as sprouting grain is to fully ripened grain. Between the one and the other there is no gap, only a boundless expansion, the swelling waters of a joy that, once it has filled the heart, flows over on all sides and covers the entire earth. The love of self in a child's heart. This is a love that flows from the source, the wellspring. It runs from childhood all the way to God. It runs from childhood, the wellspring, to God, the ocean. As for the sweetness of life, this is something that remains unchanged over the centuries. It is composed of a calm moment of a conversation, the body's repose, the color of a month of August. It is composed of the foreknowledge that one is going to live forever in the very moment in which one is living now. The love of self is the first quivering of God in the heart's rejoicing. The sweetness of life is the movement of an eternal life in the life of today.

We could just stay with that. Francis could have stayed with that, with that quivering and that movement. But this would be to reckon without events that are the hand of God placed on our hand, that imperceptibly change the writing on the page, changing the picture of our life. A breeze comes up that turns into a storm: a war breaks out between the republics of Perugia and Assisi. Francis is part of it. He cannot help being part of it. He has been dreaming for such a long time of chivalry and glory. And then, too, what a joy to come home afterwards to the young women of Assisi with scars on his body and his soul rejuvenated by battle. But as matters turn out, he will not see the young beauties of his country again for a year. He is captured and put in prison, and when he gets out he is weakened by sickness. And still full of joy. Consoling his fellow prisoners, singing on his branch as beautifully as can be. Up to this point, his cheerfulness might pass for the privilege of gilded youth, sure of its future because the master of its world. But what happens is that this state of mind persists and grows in the darkness of the prison, where he is far from his own people. Therefore this joy came from somewhere else, from much farther away than mere intoxication with the world. In the prison he is like Jonah in the belly of the whale: no brightness can reach him. So he sings. And he finds in his singing more than light and more than a world: he finds his real home, his true nature, and his true place.

We live in cities, in professions and occupations, in families. But the place we live in is not really a place like that. The place we really live in is not the one in which we pass our days, but the one in which we hope—without knowing what we are hoping for—the one in which we sing without understanding what makes us sing.

Imprisoned in 1202, freed in 1203, sick in 1204. In the period from 1202 to 1204 begins the metamorphosis of the unicorn and the salamander—into the cricket: "The nature of the cricket is to love its song and to take so much pleasure in it that it does not look for food and dies singing."

A Few Words
Full of Shadows

HE DOZES BENEATH LAYERS OF FEATH-ers and fever. He recovers gradually from his illness. The lily gets gilded a little—mother and son each find their particular pleasure in it. The mother rediscovers the immemorial gestures of the servant—a soft hand in the child's tousled hair, a hand of light on his pale heart. The son reconnects with the glory of newborn babies: a sigh capable of stirring up the entire household and alerting all the angels. His friends come to his bedside. The young ladies worry about his health. No one is sure what is the matter with him. His complexion is a bit too light, the color of milk, and then there is the brilliance in the depths of his eyes. Yes, that's what is especially amazing, the strange fire in the pupils of his eyes. A smoldering fire, you might say. Seeing it, you fear a major blaze.

He tosses and turns in his bed. He tosses and turns in his life. The sheets are rumpled, unpleasant to the touch. They chafe his skin, the creases irritate his flesh. Life is worn out, it is less pleasant to the taste, it chafes at his soul, destroys his dream. He cannot talk about it to anyone. There is nobody you can tell that you would like to leave this life for another and that you don't know how. How could you say to those close to you: your love gave me life, now it is killing me. How can you tell those who love you that they do not love you.

Three words give you fever. Three words nail you to the bed: change your life. That is the goal. It is clear and simple. But you see no road that would lead to that goal. Sickness is the absence of a road, an uncertainty about how to go on. You are not facing a question, you are on the inside of it. You are the question yourself. A new life is what you would like, but your will, which is part of your old life, has no force. You are like one of those children who have a marble in their left hand and won't let go till they have the coins they're trading it for in their right: you would like to have a new life as long as you don't lose the old one. You fear the moment of change, the moment when your hand is empty.

What is making you sick is the approach of a health that is higher than ordinary health—is incompatible with it. So fine, you resist. Everything holds you back—your mother, your friends, the young ladies. You have little affection for that life now, but at least you know what it's made of. If you leave it behind, there will be a time in which you know nothing. And it's this nothing that scares you. It's this nothing that makes you hesitate, grope, stutter—and finally go back to your old ways.

The spring of 1205. War again. There is no dearth of wars in this century. The goal of war is control of a piece of land, the acknowledgment of one master. There is only room in the world for one. I'm the master, says the Pope. It's me, says the emperor. And the struggle continues, always already provoked, impossible to end. Francis comes out of his illness in order to answer the call of the Pope. This time it must be okay: how can you fail when you have God on your side? He has himself magnificently armed, fitted out like a prince. It is a way of doing honor to his father the cloth merchant while at the same time placing himself under the Pope, who is like a distant father, one more gifted in business. Francis has the beauty of an archangel, seated on his horse ready to leave

Assisi, arrayed in a triple armor of silver, youth, and love. The people applaud him, watch him go off, perched high on the dust of the world. He has never been so beautiful, with a beauty heightened by the dangers to come. He has never been so loved. Who could wake up someone who is dreaming and triumphing in his dream? Nothing, nobody, unless perhaps another dream—which occurs during a sleep in the town of Spoleto. The chronicles say: God spoke to him and stopped him on the way. The chroniclers make people into puppets and God into a ventriloquist. Something did happen at Spoleto, doubtless. But nothing clear: neither God the Father with His drums nor the Most High with His thunder voice. It was the Most Low who whispered in the ear of the sleeper, who spoke as only He can—very low. A wisp of a dream. The twitter of a sparrow. And that is enough to cause Francis to give up his conquests and make his way back to his own country. A few words full of shadows can change a life. A mere nothing can give you to your life, a nothing can take you away from it. A nothing decides everything.

He tarries. He kills time. What else is there? The war no longer tempts him, business does not attract him. Now those are the two principal activities of men on this earth, the two sure ways to extend your name well beyond yourself. Kill without being killed, gain without losing: these two occupations dominate life. The love bond is only a variant of them. The love bond is a bond of war and a bond of business between the sexes. Or more precisely, there is no love bond because there is no love. There is no love because there is only bitterness, the bitterness of not being everything in the world, a bitterness shared equally by the emperor, the Pope, and all their subjects. Me, says the emperor. Me, says the Pope. Me, says the child when it is little. And the three—the emperor, the Pope, and the nursling—go at it to the death around the same pile of sand.

As for Francis, he has stopped talking. He sings all the time. He sings more and more. The prison of Perugia, the sickness of Assisi, and the dream of Spoleto are three discrete wounds through which the bad blood of ambition has bled away. Nothing is left but this gaiety, which is currently without an object. Being with his friends, with women, gambling, he no longer finds enough joy. Right now he hopes for a pleasure that is greater than that of being young and adored on the earth. Weeks pass. Parties follow one another and all seem alike. He still takes part but isn't

41

really there anymore. You can easily do something without being there. You can spend the best part of your life—talking, working, loving—without ever being there. Finally one day, a soft day in the summer of 1205, he lays on an even more sumptuous banquet than usual. A magical meal, magnificent, the last of its kind. This is the way he takes leave of those close to him, amid the partying crowd, turning to them his brightest face, his body already half engaged in the night.

He is not abandoning the wedding party to go cover himself with ashes. He is not exchanging the dew of the bodies of young women for the gargoyle rain of the cathedrals. It is not the world he is leaving behind, it is himself.

He's going where singing never runs out of breath, where the world is nothing more than a single elemental note held infinitely, a single string of light vibrating eternally in everything, everywhere.

He disappears from the town. He is like someone hiding a mistress. But he doesn't find his mistress right away. He looks for her in the abandoned churches that he restores with his own hands. The word is in him, an order has finally been given: "Go and repair my house, which has fallen into ruins."

The naive youth believes that the house of God is the Church. He obeys like a child—literally, conscientiously. He moves the old stones about. He sweeps out chapels that no one visits anymore except fairies and field mice. The dust gets under his fingernails. Weariness gets into his muscles. A good little mason, living on song and fresh water.

He travels again, makes journeys that are the opposite of the earlier ones—no glory, no weapons, no publicity. He goes to Rome because it is far away—no one knows him there. He hangs around the beggars the way in the old days he used to linger near the most beautiful of the young women. He is like a dog scenting game. He is not seeking poverty. He is seeking the abundance that no amount of money can provide. He instinctively guesses that the truth is to be found much more in the low than in the high, much more in dearth than in plenty. And what is the truth? The truth is nothing outside of us. The truth is not in the knowledge we have of it but in the joy that it gives us. The truth is a joy of a kind that nothing can dispel, a treasure that even death—that thieving magpie—is incapable of taking away. And he is very close to it. He knows it, he feels it. But there is still a shadow between him and his joy, between the world

43

as illuminated by God and the world as it burns in his heart. A final holding back that he formulates very astutely, with the precision of a mason passing his hand over an invisible crack—a fault in the soul, a break in the voice of a singer: "At that time I found it extremely bitter to see lepers." Poverty in its material nakedness attracts him. Poverty in its fleshly truth fills him with loathing. There is still this point in the world that his joy does not reach. And what is a joy that leaves something outside of it? Nothing. Less than nothing. A love that is no more than lip service. A love without love. A feeling that is crumbly, porous—like all feelings. Middle-class people dream of poor people who conform to their interests. Priests dream of poor people who conform to their hopes. Francis, however, is not dreaming, not anymore. He sees: poverty is not a lovable thing. A defect, a misery, a wound, yes. But nothing lovable. No one is naturally worthy of love, neither the rich person nor the poor person. By nature, love does not exist—it is just some murky water in a mirror, a momentary alliance of two interests, a mixture of war and business. What is natural is the kind of love that resembles you, that flatters you—warm friends, perfumed ladies. What is supernatural is to go into the house of the lepers near Assisi, to go through one room after the other, walking with a peasant's step, being suddenly calm, suddenly at peace, seeing coming toward you those rags of flesh, those filthy hands that fall on your shoulders, grope at your face; it is to contemplate these phantoms and hug them to your body, for a long time, in silence, obviously in silence: you would not want to talk about God to these people. They are from the world's other side. They are the refuse of the world, excluded from the pleasures of the living as well as from the repose of the dead. They have enough of a sense of the world to understand where the young man's gesture comes from, to understand that it is not coming from him but from God. Only the Most Low can bow so deeply with so much simple grace.

He comes out of there with a fever in his heart and a blush on his cheeks. Or rather, he does not come out of there; he never will come out of there again. He has found his master's house. He now knows where the Most Low dwells: down at the level where the worldly light shines, where life does without everything, where life is life at its crudest—an elemental wonder, a destitute miracle.

Look at Me:
I Am about to Leave

THERE IS A TIME WHEN THE PARENTS nurture a child, and there is a time when they prevent it from nurturing itself. The child is the only one capable of distinguishing between these two times, the only one who can draw the logical conclusion: leave. Do not struggle. Especially, do not struggle—leave. Nothing is more formidable for a son than carrying on a campaign of resistance, spirit against spirit, with his father. To oppose someone is more or less to take on his qualities. Sons who strengthen themselves on a struggle with their fathers end up strangely resembling them in the evening of their lives.

Francis of Assisi, with a sure instinct, catches the occasion of the legal action his father brings against him on the fly. It is a real lawsuit, brought against the son in order to disinherit him and make him give back some money from the shop that he has given without authorization to some priests. Suits brought by fathers against their sons are usually cloaked affairs, cases that creep along, indefinitely prolonged beneath the surface of the passing days, difficult to formulate, difficult to bring to an end. But this one happens in broad daylight, in front of the bishop and the good people assembled as witnesses to the paternal wrath.

Francis of Assisi does not say anything on that day. He has no need to say anything in order to be heard. A gesture does the job. The father's speech is harsh, imperious. His son's silence responds to it point by point, defeats it word by word.

"Look. Look at the flesh of your flesh, the blood of your blood. Have a good look at me, a good long look, you whose eyes are almost closed as though against the gusting of the light, your cunning eyes, squinting, blinded by the desire not to miss anything in the world, the desire to see everything that belongs to them by right, yes, look at me as long as you like with your eyes of a merchant considering fine fabric, with your eyes of a male shining at the sight of a good-looking woman. Look at me with your father's eyes. Father Bernardone and son Francis. You are my father, and I am no longer your son Francis. I am going back to the name that got covered up, the one my mother wanted to give me, the one that you buried under the good earth of France, which was such a delight to your heart, so fertile for your business. I do not hold it against you. I do not hold anything against you, and doubtless that is the very thing that separates us. I do not hold it against you that you consigned the name John to oblivion. That which is banished is protected by that banishment. That name is still there. I rediscover it today, ready to be used. John who watches over the song of the world. John who has a golden bird in the cage of his voice. John who keeps the sun like a big, old faithful dog. John the Baptist and John the Evangelist. You know the beginning of his book: In the beginning was the Word, and the Word was with God, and the Word was in God, and the Word was God.* What could the beginning be for people like you: the first money that came in, the first girl rolled in the grass? For me the beginning is there in God's silence, in this power of the Word. You are my father. You are not my father except starting from the beginning of my

*See John 1:1–2.

49

days—and that is a very short time. I take everything starting from well before you, from farther upstream. I am beating my way back like a salmon toward the eternal waters. I am going to slip in between two things—between the drunken word and the silent God. There is no space between the two, no distance whatsoever, but I will find a way to slip in, to give my soul the required thinness, the necessary humility. Humility. Do you know the origin of this word? My Latin teacher taught it to me. Listen, you will not have paid for those lessons in vain; listen to how simple it is. *Humility* comes from the Latin *humus*, which means "earth," "the earth." Well, that is what I am going back to, that is the direction I am going in, toward my sister the earth, toward my lover the earth. You did well to provide me with this second name, Francis. From the first name I received seriousness; from this one I received joy, without which seriousness is nothing but weight. Yes, you did well, you lived up well to your role of father. It is good for a child to have both his parents; each one protects him from the other. The father saves him from an overdevouring mother, the mother saves him from an overauthoritarian father. I have nothing to reproach you with, but right now it is necessary for me to leave you, to go do the work of my father—not the one who sells cloth to rich people but the one whose business is the rain, the snow, and laughter. And it is necessary for me to go do the work of my mother— not the one who prefers her eldest son to the other children of the neighborhood but the one who shows the same toughness and the same sweetness to everybody, my mother the earth, my mother the sky. You understand what I am saying to you, what I am telling you without saying a word, through my silence before you and the bishop, through my joy that is almost irrepressible on this day in court. You understand: I am not opposing you. For me to oppose you there would have to be a common household, a common language, interests in common, and we have none of all that. You have just decided that yourself, so that will be the last help you give me, your last work as my father. The suit you have brought against me frees me of you. In this you have completed your work of progenitor; in this, that work reaches perfection, before these dignitaries who accompany you, beneath the purple of the law that you embody. The father is he who proclaims the law. But tell me, what kind of father is it who subordinates himself like a little boy to the law of money, to the law of solemnity,

to the law of the dead world? And why all this com-
motion? For a few coins that I took out of your cash
drawer and donated to a priest for repairs to his
church? And this priest did not even want them. He
threw them in the dust out of fear of you and your
almighty name. The priest too, that dealer in eternal
underwear, that dealer in prayers and communion
wafers, he too did me a fine favor. He showed me
without knowing it that what is necessary is not to
give money but one's life, and that it must be given
not to those who make a profession of talking about
it in their masses, but to those who do not even have
a tongue left to moan with. Take a look at me, I am
about to leave. The priest was afraid of you, and you,
you were afraid of losing your money. The mouse is
afraid of the cat, and the cat is afraid of the dog. This
is the way you all go round and round, sweating under your morals, trembling with fear under your
principles. In the beginning was fear, and fear was
with the law, and fear was your only law. Take a look
at me, I am about to leave. I am not going to genu-
flect anymore before your laws. I have found my only
master. I am going to put your business know-how to
good use. I am going to deal with the eternal without
a middleman; I am going to invest my soul to the last

penny and get the whole of creation in return. What a splendid piece of business: on one side the counterfeit money of my blood, on the other side, all the love in the world. I will be rich in an entirely different way from you. I will be enriched by everything that I lose. The world of the spirit is nothing different from the material world. The world of the spirit is just the material world finally set right. In the world of the spirit, one makes one's fortune by going bankrupt. Take a look at me, I am about to leave. You will have to find somebody else to take over the shop and your name, to perpetuate the old story. Your father was in business. In going into business in your turn, you obeyed him, you gave up growing up. I have meditated a lot on this—oh, not by reading books, you know that. Reading is not my strong point. I am not a monk, gorged on beautiful inks; illumination is not my thing. But I have looked around and seen what happens to the sons of good families after they pass through the romping bedlam of their twenties. I have seen that they take over their father's seat. I have seen that they take over everything of their father's, up to and including the wrinkles on his face. With such poverty of invention, there is no hope for a man. They think they are becoming mature because they have children. They think they love, because they no longer dare to deceive their wives. They will never have done anything but get old. They will never have done anything but be old. Take a look at me, I am about to depart on the pathways of childhood. I owe you a few pennies, which I took to throw at God. You who know the prices of things, you who know nothing about things except their prices, look here. I am taking off my clothes, I am stripping here in front of you, in front of the bishop and all these well-off people. Look at the pile this makes on this stone floor. Weigh it up, calculate. Consider yourself reimbursed. I no longer owe you a thing. Therefore, I may depart, naked as a stone, naked as a blade of grass, naked as the first star in the black sky. Abraham arose. He was called upon infinitely. He was called upon to leave his family, his country, his friends. Anyone who desires with an infinite desire is always called upon infinitely. And Abraham arose and departed. And Moses and David and all of them arose, and in the act of arising they lost their clothing of language, their clothing of friendship, their clothing of wisdom, and all of them received the infinite into their denuded hearts. To his mother who urged him to come back home because she was ashamed to see him on the tramp with these twelve ne'er-do-wells, Christ replied: Where is my real family, which ones are mine? And his mother failed to understand, so how could you understand: I am going back to my real family. I am rejoining those who left without knowing anymore who they were or where they were going. O my businessman father, O my father who wants to keep me from growing up, do you know how much violence it takes to be able to enjoy the true sweetness, do you know that your son is crazy with crazy sweetness? This is no figment of the imagination that I am embracing. It is not purity that I want. Purity leaves impurity out; I want nothing more to do with a church that has its angels in the choir and its devils on the street, their faces pressed against the stained glass like poor people at Christmastime with their faces against the baker's window. I no longer want anything to do with anything but the life that is naked and brotherly. O my reasonable father, O my reason-wielding father, you were taught that there was a place for everything, and you believed, for that reason, that there is a rank and position for everyone, and I have come to tell you no. We will not be properly ranked except in heaven. Until that day, which will come, which will necessarily come, which will come without a doubt—until that day when we will be squeezed against God's bosom like pennies at the bottom of a pocket, I want to pass beyond all the cloistered gardens, jump over all the stone walls, go everywhere in splendid disorder. Yesterday I dreamed of princesses and knights. Today I have found something greater than my dream. Love has awakened my sleeping life. I have found life, I am leaving to go to that life, I will do battle for that life, and I will serve its name. I am leaving—what can you do against that? I am leaving you my clothes down to the last garment. We keep our hold on people by what we give them. I have given you back what you gave me—all except for my life. But life comes to me from more than you. Life comes to me from life, and it is toward that that I am going, toward my lover with the eyes of snow, my little wellspring, my only wife. Life, nothing but life. Life, all of life.

Young man, going naked far from his father. Childhood dancing lightly on the poor earth."

A little while later, a phrase from the gospels makes the decision about what clothes he is going to wear. Certainly, it is necessary to wear something.

The seasons are sometimes harsh for human beings, and the earth is not always a garden of delights.

The son of the merchant of fine fabrics will wear a tunic of low-quality cloth with a rope for a belt.

Four Thousand Years and a Little Dust

A FEW HOURS AFTER THE COURT proceedings, he meets a beggar and asks him for the blessing that his father has refused him. Now he will really be able to go, having taken on a real kinship: the real father is the one who blesses, not the one who curses. The real father is one who opens up avenues with his word, not one who holds his child in the nets of his resentment.

Francis goes into the forest and constructs a lean-to out of ferns and branches. The way you see him there, kneeling on the stones or stretched out in the grass, praying or sleeping—yes, the way you see him there, he is four thousand years old. Four thousand years old plus a little dust. He comes in a straight line from Abraham. His cousins, his nephews, and his uncles are there with him, recorded in the Bible, where they recite a psalm of King David, the beloved secretary of God Almighty.

At this moment two careers are open to him, that of a madman or that of a saint. At the beginning, the difference between the two is nonexistent. It is only later that it develops, only later can it be seen. To begin with, the madman and the saint resemble each other like twin brothers. To begin with, they both speak the truth. Only later do things start to go bad. The madman, in proclaiming the truth, makes it refer back to himself, wrings a profit from it. The saint, in proclaiming the truth, refers it on the spot to its true addressee, like someone adding a missing address to an envelope. "I speak the truth, therefore I am not mad," says the madman. "I speak the truth, but I am not true," says the saint. "I am not holy," says the saint, "only God is holy. I refer you to Him." The madmen and the saints are often to be found side by side in history. They pass close to each other, search each other out, and sometimes they meet each other; for the madman, this is the greatest possible misfortune, his grandest calamity. Three of the four Evangelists describe Christ's healing of a possessed man "who had his dwelling among the tombs; and no one could bind him, no, not even with a chain."* The madman is in the company of the dead. He has his face turned toward the shadow. Nothing reaches him any longer except from the past. He cannot connect with anything or with anybody, he cannot enter into any living relationship with the living. The saint has his face turned like the prow of a ship toward what is coming from the future to fecundate the present— the pollen of God transported by all kinds of angels. The saint never comes to the end of connecting the close with the faraway, the human with the divine, the living with the living.

"And my hand hath found as a nest the riches of the people: and as one gathereth eggs that are left, have I gathered all the earth." This is the great prophet Isaiah speaking, in the Bible.† This is the reaper Isaiah, pushing before him the cart of his voice, filled with gold and fire. This is the peacock Isaiah, flourishing his plumage behind a grillwork of ink. This is Isaiah tossing the mane of his voice, and this is God roaring, a jealous God, a God sick with jealousy, a God worse than a devil, a God like a child

---

*See Mark 5:3.   †Isaiah 10:14.

who holds the speckled egg of the world in the hollow of his hands and at intervals squeezes it in his fingers, squeezes it to the point where his joints whiten, and does not ease his pressure until the last second, just before the first cracks in the shell. The Bible says that man was made in the image of God—and it is true that man and God resemble each other even in their anger. It is difficult for man to love without bitterness, and it is almost as difficult for God. How is it possible not to give up on this dubious mixture of clay and spirit, on this heart full of slime and noise? For, at last, in the ultimate end, who was it who conceived of these wonders turned to garbage, what mason built this house soiled by its inhabitants? "Who hath wrought and done it, calling the generations from the beginning? I the Lord, the first, and with the last; I am he."* This is the juggler Isaiah spitting the fire of the Word. This is Isaiah the bear trainer, and this is God dancing, breaking His chains, drunk with fury, a terrible fury, comparable only to that of a small child, impossible to pacify at that moment, inaccessible to the voices that would appease it. This is God enraged over His rights: they

*Isaiah 41:4.

owe everything to Me. Without Me, there would have been nothing but mucky earth, desolate marshes. Without the fire of My breath in their damp veins, like the flesh of reeds, they would never have known the drunkenness of having a life and not knowing what to do with it. The imbeciles: a life is made to be given—and for nothing else. They owe me everything, and here, just barely having been born, still teetering on their legs, they turn away from me, they foul my breath with their black exhalations, they separate my breath from their breath and then are nothing more than dry clay, wineskins filled with vinegar, funerary vases full of mud. This is Isaiah rapping the world on its head with the stick of his voice, this is Isaiah and this is God when God is like Father Bernardone, when He clings to his souls the way the other one clings to His pennies; when he does his accounts and they don't come out right, he yells, he howls, he curses, and asks himself what he has done to deserve children like that. This is Isaiah and God at the beginning of the world, at the time of the first steps of God on the earth. Human beings at the beginning had a bit of a hard time getting used to God. At the beginning God had a bit of a hard time getting used to human beings. And in the thirteenth century we are still back at the beginning. In the twentieth century we are no further along; we have hardly done more than move our feet and get ourselves stuck a little deeper in this furor in the mirror that goes on between God and human beings—witness the dust on our shoes and the blood in dry scales on our fancy outfits.

Francis of Assisi knows Isaiah and the whole gang of prophets, those dogs of the Book gnawing on bones of fire, those angels sprawling in the grass of a voice. He knows the Bible well from having heard it frequently. He knows that it is a book of the Word: what is said is said. You cannot add anything to it, you cannot subtract anything. The laughter of the simple folk and the floury faces of the sages, the net for catching the phosphorescent fish of the soul, the sword of the Last Judgment for slicing up the world like a piece of butter, the lost lamb for which a herd of a thousand head is neglected, and Solomon and Moses and Jacob and Abel, and the whores and the queens and the madwomen, and the shepherds and the magi and the kings—all of those have been cited, all have borne witness in the trial opposing God to His creation, all of them have been heard, everything has been said once and for all, and there is nothing to add. You only have to follow along, let yourself be carried by the breath of the Word, more fiery than the breath of a bomb. The voice of God is in the Bible under the tons of ink, like the concentrated energy under tons of concrete at a nuclear power plant. The young man of Assisi is irradiated by that voice. He no longer wants anything but to transmit it, without changing a comma. You can look for Francis of Assisi in Isaiah. You will find him there. He is there as he is everywhere in the Book: never will a man so completely attune his life to the Word as he did, never will a man so let his breath become one with the breath of God. But you will not find him in the stormy passages of the Bible, rather where it murmurs like a lover to his beloved: "No more shall you be named 'Forsaken,' nor your land be named 'Desolate'; but you shall be called 'My delight is in her,' and your land 'Married.'"* Or in this, also from Isaiah, which will serve him as a motto: "The living, the living, he alone shall praise thee."† He has no taste for curses; that is a taste of the weak. His voice is calm, so calm that it causes the poor people to come closer who have never gotten anything from the world but a

*Isaiah 62:4.   †Isaiah 38:19.

bark. He adopts the voice of the Most Low, never that of the Most High. He knows very well that there is only one God. Though he may prefer the infinite sweetness to infinite anger, he knows very well that both come from the same sole infinite—that of love. He knows all that very well, but he prefers this way of doing things. It comes to him from childhood, from his first years, spent in God's lap, under his mother's skirts.

The prophets address human beings in order to speak to them about God, which is what gives their voices that raucous timbre and dusky coloring. But Francis addresses God in order to talk to Him about human beings, to cause to ring in the ear of this distant God the pure note that each person gives out with his life, merely by maintaining his life through time. It is a light note, a reedy note. You have to speak as softly as possible in order not to drown it out.

His mother smiles to him from a distance, from over yonder. The mother is victorious in her pain. By her side is a man who is brewing up his wrath, a merchant sure of his duty, a father certain he has been offended and that the offense is unpardonable. There are the two of them in their bed, the father and the mother. There are only the two of them in the house. The mother goes off in her sleep to join her disinherited son, the strange adolescent, the troubadour baby. What she started with him—what all mothers since the beginning of the world start again and again without ever being able to complete it— her boy is going to finish off, enlarge, and perfect, leaning over the crib of the world, imposing silence on the powerful, on merchants, on warriors, on priests, and even on God. Yes, even on God the Most High, who talks too loud, much too loud, in children's bedrooms.

Brother Ass

A SPARROW SPEAKS: "I AM A BREAD crumb in Christ's beard, a snippet of his speech, enough to nourish the world until the end of the world."

A robin redbreast speaks: "I am a wine spot on Christ's shirt, a burst of his laughter at the return of springtime."

A lark speaks: "I am Christ's last sigh, I ascend directly to heaven, I knock with my beak on the clear blue sky, I ask to be let in, I bring the whole earth along in my song, I ask, I ask, I ask."

All of them, male and female, twitter and sing in this way and come to know the truth of their song in the presence of Francis of Assisi, in the presence of the tree man, the flower man, the wind man, the earth man.

The birds were the first occupants of the Bible,

well before the appearance of humans, just after God's awakening. You open the Book to its first page and right away there is this racket, thousands of birds in God's fire, thousands of wings beating in the panic of love. You enter the Bible via Genesis. In Genesis you are as though in God's rib cage, on the level of His diaphragm: with each tide of breath the world rises, entire layers of the world rise up, first the waters, then the areas of land, then the rocks and the plants, then the animals, and finally, at the end of the breathing, human beings—and then, too, this amazing thing, the enigma of God's ignorance with regard to His creation. For God who makes everything knows nothing about what He makes. God, who made the animals, does not know their names: "And out of the ground the Lord God formed every beast of the field, and every fowl of the air; and brought them unto Adam to see what he would call them: and whatsoever Adam called every living creature, that was the name thereof."* In the presence of God, the beasts lived far from their names. And they still retain within them something of this first silence. On the one side, they are like God; on the other, they are

*Genesis 2:19.

70

like humans. They wander back and forth, timidly, between the two. Francis of Assisi goes back to these beginnings in preaching to the birds. In giving them a name, man enclosed them in his own history, in the curse of his life and his death. In speaking to them of God, Francis liberates them from this destiny, returns them to the absolute, from which everything escaped as from an open birdcage.

He speaks to the swallows and converses with the wolves. He enters into union with the rocks and organizes conferences with the trees. He talks with the whole universe, for in love everything has the power of speech. Everything is endowed with meaning in his crazy love.

He is Christian, therefore he is Jewish. The Bible is his family album. He is related to his Jewish ancestors, who are in the Bible: he moves in the world as in an obscure book. He moves with patience from the nothingness of one letter to the nothingness of the following letter, and the whole thing ends up a single sentence, clean and clear. He speaks with sweetness to each ephemeral life and gathers them all into an eternity of prevailing love.

The Jewish people is a people that God invented for Himself in the pain of His love, a people only for

Himself. For centuries He moved the lantern of His voice around on the earth, in the region of marshes, at the bottoms of caves; for centuries He searched for human beings who might possibly respond to His love, to His madness, and since He found none, He invented them. He took them from the lowest part of opulent Egypt: they were slaves, shadows. One by one He gathered them under the wings of His voice and said to them: I have placed my heart in a faraway country, in a land of springs and olive trees, which is only for you. I will lead you there, I will take you there, to the promised land.

And off they go. They start out on the way, departing from Egypt and walking in file through the desert, in columns of black sentences in the Bible. When they raise their heads, they sense the length of the way, the thickness of the Book, and sometimes they stop, make a fire, pitch their tents. They stop on ten pages for ten years. God is not in these parts of the Book anymore. God is no longer there to continue writing the story of love, the terrible story of His love for some shadows. In these moments, what dominates is fatigue. It falls on the napes of their necks like lead. It is not the going from one chapter to the next that is tiring. What is tiring is hope. So sometimes they fall into despair. Not a step further. It is out of the question to take one more step. They curse God, then they get tired of cursing Him. They adopt another god, one more to their taste. Anything can serve as God when God is missing. So then God—the real one, the one who loves them like a madman, who counts them one by one—God comes and pulls up the stakes of their tents, yanks them out of their cozy bed of despair by the hair, and off they go once again among the sand dunes, along the lines full of ink. Old people die, children are born. Time passes. When you turn a page in the Bible, a century falls, a century or two. They arrive, exhausted, thin, at the beginning of the fourth chapter of Numbers. They are in the country of Moab. The king of Moab wants no part of these people in his country. He has read the preceding pages, the ones where he was reigning. He is afraid of these people. He calls upon Balaam, a magus who has the power of the curse; his voice holds thunder. Initially, Balaam refuses. Then he says what people always say when they have already chosen in the depths of their souls and are talked into hesitating again. He says, "Let's go see these Jews, and we'll make up our minds on the spot." But his mind is made up, his will to do harm is already there. And that is the point at which God intervenes—not God himself but a proxy, an ass; more precisely, a female ass. She takes Balaam on the road that leads in the direction of the Jewish people. An angel appears in the middle of the road brandishing a sword. Balaam sees nothing. The ass, who sees the angel, turns aside and goes off into a field. The second time, the angel takes his stance across a narrow pathway with a wall to the right and a wall to the left. The ass gets past by scraping along the wall. Balaam curses at having his leg bruised on the stones. The third time the angel with the sword appears, there is no space at all to go forward. The ass lies down. Balaam beats her. Then the ass speaks. She recounts her visions of the angel: three times God has shown his will to prevent Balaam from doing his dirty work. It is only then that Balaam understands and gives up obstructing the advance of the shadows toward the fifth chapter, the next desert.*

From this story we can conclude two things. The first is that asses see angels, and that shouldn't surprise us. It is enough to see these inglorious beasts, their eyes blanked by weariness, and their ears, espe-

*This story about Balaam appears in Numbers 22–24.

cially their ears, their poor spoiled ears, half broken
down, often gnawed by a badly healed wound; yes, it
is enough to see these bags of bones and hair to understand that such disgrace could not fail to attract
the bountiful grace of the angels, just as necessarily
as a magnet attracts iron filings. The second thing we
learn from this story is that the truth can quite easily
come out of the mouth of an ass, and this too should
not surprise us. The truth owes nothing to the sup-
posed greatness of our fortunes or our minds. The
light of the truth is in itself, not in the person who
says it. It is great, when it is, only through its prox-
imity to life that is poor and weak. The idiot of
Nazareth knew this well, astride a young ass at the
gates of Jerusalem, anointed king by the crowd a few
hours before being put to death by it: the truth is
never so great as in the humiliation of the one who
proclaims it.

That makes four of them now on the roads of Assisi: Tobias's dog, the angel, and the child, which, out
of breath from the walk, has just climbed up on the
back of Balaam's ass. Four, not counting the deafening swarms of birds in the skies all around.

And yes, there is an ass in the life of Francis, too. It
sleeps when Francis sleeps, it eats when Francis eats,

it prays when Francis prays. It never leaves him; it accompanies him from the first day to the last day. It is the body of Francis of Assisi, his own body, which he refers to as "my brother the ass." This is a way of being detached from it without rejecting it, because it is with this companion that you have to go to heaven, with this impatient flesh and these burdensome desires: there is no other access to the eternal summits but that path there, steep and stony—a real donkey's path.

Men follow the animals to Francis's side. Before long there are a dozen of them who believe the unbelievable, and twelve is already quite a lot. For them he devises a rule, which he presents to the Pope so that the latter can stamp it in good and due form. For he does not seek the role of master, which is the role of good students. He does not want to found a new church. As he sees it, there are too many churches already. "Let the brothers be careful absolutely not to accept churches, poor dwellings, or anything that may be built for them if it does not conform to the holy poverty to which we are pledged in the rule, sheltering in it always as strangers and pilgrims." I am obedient to your Church, Most High Pope, but I will never be anything more in it than a transient, like a stranger or a pilgrim: there could be no more delicate manner of bringing together the most painstaking obedience with the most sovereign liberty.

"And Adam gave names to all cattle, and to the fowl of the air, and to every beast of the field; but for Adam there was not found a help meet for him. And the Lord God caused a deep sleep to fall upon Adam, and he slept; and He took one of his ribs, and closed up the flesh instead thereof."*

For man to know himself, more than a name was necessary: an absence from himself, a "deep sleep" followed by having something ripped out of him—from which he received a woman. The final flowering of the genesis, the ultimate point of the Creation.

And we must admit that, although animals and men have started to approach Francis of Assisi, this story is still missing a woman—she who, in carrying out the task of a mother, completes and perfects the work of God himself.

*Genesis 2:20–21.

The Women's Camp, the Camp of God's Laughter

MEN ARE AFRAID OF WOMEN. IT IS A fear that comes to them from as far away as their life does. It is a fear there from the first day that is not merely fear of the body, of the face, and of the heart of a woman, but is also fear of life and fear of God. For those three are very close to each other—woman, life, and God. What is a woman? No one knows how to answer this question, not even God, even though He knows them through having been born to one. Women are not God. Women are not *completely* God. They are just a little short of it. Much less so than men. Women are life in the sense that life is the closest thing to the laughter of God. Women watch over life in God's absence, they are in charge of the clear feeling of ephemeral life, the fundamental sensation of eternal life. And men—unable to get beyond their fear of women, believing they get beyond it through seduction, through war, or through work, but never really getting beyond it, having an eternal fear of women—condemn themselves eternally to know almost nothing about them, to taste almost nothing of life and of God. Because it is the men who create churches, it is inevitable that churches mistrust women, just as, in fact, they mistrust God, trying to tame the former and the latter, trying to contain a life in spate within the prudent bed of precepts and rites. In this respect the Church of Rome resembles all the others. In 1310, less than a century after the death of Francis of Assisi, it burned a woman, Marguerite Porete, for her book *The Mirror of Simple and Annihilated Souls.* In this book there is nothing that Francis of Assisi could not have undersigned, nothing more than he said without saying it—in his singing. In this book, she does not draw upon the Latin of the priests but rather upon the Provençal of the troubadours, a language of sparrows and princes, a half-starved language of the overabundance of love. She addresses herself neither to the Most High nor to the Most Low. She speaks to the Far-Near. She speaks to God, giving Him the name that all wives could give their husbands: the

Far-near. Neither never there nor never elsewhere. Neither really absent nor really present. At the same time as her flesh, a sentence from Marguerite Porete's book shriveled at the stake, consumed by the flames without losing anything of its transparency: "One cannot say of anyone that he is insignificant, because he is called to see God without end." This sentence, which took flight in the hot air and whirled above the Place de Grève on that lovely June day in 1310, was swallowed by the sky and fell back less than a century earlier to settle on the coarse cloth of the sleeve of Francis of Assisi: he never said anything different. He never experienced anything that was not in perfect accord with this belief in the absolute equality of every living being with all the others, with the same dignity of existence allotted to each one— beggars, burghers, trees, or stones—solely in virtue of the miracle of having appeared on the earth, all bathed in the same sun of sovereign love. For this belief, the one was canonized, the other burned—and in the end both are part of the same misunderstanding. The word of adoration, like the word of malediction, is completely ignorant of what it names, and moreover, the two sometimes succeed each other with only a second's interval on the same lips, in reference to the same object, in reference to the same person.

The difference between men and women is not a difference of sex but of place. The man stays in his man's place, cleaves to it ponderously, with seriousness, remains safely within his fear. The woman does not remain in any place, not even her own, but constantly disappears into the love that she calls, calls, calls. This difference would be a desperate one if it were not for the fact that it can be overcome at any moment. The man, who does not know anything about women other than the fear they inspire in him and who thus knows nothing at all, nevertheless has a first hint of light, a fragment of what God is, in his melancholy at the laughter of women, in his invincible nostalgia for a face illuminated by carefreeness. It is always possible for a man to join the camp of the women, of the laughter of God. A movement is all it takes, a single movement of the sort that children make when they throw themselves forward with all their might and without any fear of falling or dying, forgetting the weight of the world. A man who departs from himself like that, who departs from his fear, neglecting that weight of seriousness that is the

82

weight of the past, is a man who no longer keeps to his place, who no longer believes in the inevitabilities dictated by gender, in the hierarchies imposed by law or custom. He is a child or a saint in the laughing presence of God—and of women. And on this point the Church of Rome distinguishes itself from all the others: no one turned his face toward women more than Christ did, as one turns to look at some greenery, as one leans over the waters of a river to draw strength from them and a taste for continuing on the way. Women are almost as numerous in the Bible as birds. They are there at the beginning and they are there at the end. They bring God into the world, they watch Him grow up, play, die; then they bring Him back to life with simple gestures of crazy love, the same gestures since the beginning of the world, in the caves of prehistory and in the overheated rooms of maternity wards.

In his naive, almost manic imitation of the Scriptures, Francis of Assisi could not avoid this encounter with a loving woman—his sister, his double. There is nothing to say about her, except that they complement each other like the two pillars of a rainbow, all the nuances of love passing from one to the other, all the colors of dreams. There is nothing to say about her other than her name, and her name says what she is: Clare—clear. A clearing in the woods, a clearstory, clairvoyance, a flash of clarity, a clearing in the weather—all these things are in her name, all these lights come from her, a girl of sixteen whom her parents want to marry off, a girl like those in the old French songs, a bird who rebels against the song she is taught, a sparrow who would rather hop along the roads beaten with rain than languish in the branches of a single tree—even if it is a tree of high lineage. "What do you want to do later on?" they say to this child who does not know what "later on" means, who knows nothing but the present, the miraculous presence of everything. Whom do you want to marry later on? they ask this girl whose beauty disquiets and argues to have an end put to it by marriage. For marriages wear out love, tire it out, draw it into the seriousness and weight that is the place of the world. But the one she wants to marry is not there and never will be. He is not there and he is not somewhere else. He is most high and he is most low, he is far and near. He does not fall into any inevitability of history, he falls into no rancor for love lost, he cannot be lost and he cannot be gained, he is and he is not. As in the old songs, the girl leaves her parents' house at night, escapes through a hidden door that is blocked by a huge pile of wood. She moves the logs one by one with her own hands and flees into the starry night to the one who planned the kidnapping, the king of her heart, the prince of runaways, Francis of Assisi. They love with the same love, they were made to understand one another, they are drunk on the same wine. She exchanges her sparkling gown for a coarse woolen smock, and there the two of them are for years, together and separate, he catching with the snare of his voice the birds of the heavens, the beasts of the field, and the men of the towns, and she chasing girls into God's nets, more and more of them, more and more beautiful ones.

Two poachers. Two nomads on the invisible estates of God.

Separated as children used to be in the old days in little schools. She on the girls' side, he on the boys'. Separated in appearances and in places. United by the care of souls without end, by the rapture of having found the optimal partner, he who hears everything and she who hears everything, hears even the silences, even what one could never find a way of saying to oneself in the silence. The sister and the brother without whom the time that has passed on earth would be only time, nothing more.

The legend that tells the truth—not truth the way it is in the deadliness of proofs but the way it is in the blood of souls—that legend says that one day when Francis was visiting Clare and her sisters in the convent, a fire occurred, seen for several leagues around. The people of Assisi came running to put it out and found no flame, no fire whatsoever. Just Francis of Assisi and Clare sitting at a meager meal and a great light between them, radiance impossible to diminish.

He will die before her, and this is of no importance, because from the moment it first arrived, from the moment of its first thrill, love abolished the ancient decrees of time, did away with the distinctions of before and after, and maintained only the eternal today of the living, the tender today of love.

That Anachronism, God

HE SEDUCES WITH HIS VOICE. WITH his voice of flesh, he attracts wolves and men who are worse than wolves. But how should we hear this angelic breath of the flesh, this carnal voice of the soul, seven centuries later? It was extinguished with the body that bore it. The song disappeared with the bird. Oh, we have kept a few feathers, some relics. The wool from a piece of clothing, the shell of a skull. But the voice is gone for good. No more bird, no more song. What remains is the light in which the song wandered, this inexhaustible light of every day of our lives, the same light down through the centuries, and the name, so old, of this light that is so young, this name, which is blind in all languages, this innocence in all voices—God. What remains is God, the old sun by which everything can be awakened—both the bird and the song.

If we want to know a man, we have to look for the one toward whom his life is secretly directed, the one to whom he speaks in preference to all others, even when he seems to be speaking to us. Everything depends on this other whom he has chosen for himself. Everything depends on the one to whom he addresses himself in silence, for whose consideration he has accumulated facts and proofs, for the love of whom he has made his life what it is. For most people, there will be only a single interlocutor: the father or the mother, figures who rule through their absence, who crush their child's life with the full weight of what they were incapable of giving. Look at what I am doing. It is for you. It is to win your love, it is so you will finally turn your eyes on me, so that with the full light of your eyes you will endow me with the certainty that I exist. Many people are thralls to a shadow in this way, shut up in their father's garden, in their mother's bedroom, continuing into the twilight of their lives their supplications to the absent one. Francis of Assisi is not, is no longer, one of these people. He came to the end of the endless story with the father on the day of the lawsuit, in effect through the nakedness of being reborn, of being liberated from the old habits of a son. Naked flesh, pure soul. I strip myself of everything in order to get free of you. I show myself as you did not make me: weak with the weakness that eludes your power, against which you can no longer do a thing. I return to that God of which you are no more than an image, deceptive like all images. That father will make a much lighter one than you. He watches me come and go. In His absences, He is far less devastating than you are. In His presence, He allows me much more play than you do. He does not believe in money as you do, in duty, in seriousness. Moreover, He spends all His time in the useless company of children, dogs, and asses.

Mothers love their children insanely. Mothers do not know how to love except in this insane manner. They keep their children at the center of the world and the world in the center of their heart. Francis of Assisi freed himself from his mother by not resisting her, by carrying the burn of her love everywhere in the world, in which henceforth there was nothing but centers, nothing but only children, the sons of queens. My sister the river, my brother the wind, my sister the star, my brother the tree: everything is put by him, put back by him, where it should be: in the intensity of a single origin, put back in the hands of an immense demented mother, eternally anxious for her offspring, eternally in love with time.

God. That anachronism, God, that old candle, God, burning in the darkness of the centuries, that blood-red will-o'-the-wisp, that pitiful bit of a candle blown out by all the winds—we the people of the twentieth century do not know what to do with it. We are people of reason. We are adults. We no longer light by candle. We once hoped that churches would deliver us from God—they were made for that. Religions didn't bother us. Religions are weighty and that weight was rather reassuring. It is lightness that terrifies us, that lightness of God in God, of the spirit in the spirit. And anyhow, we have left the churches. We have come a long way. From childhood to adulthood, from error to truth. Nowadays we know where the truth lies. It lies in sex, in the economy, and in culture. And we know well where the truth of this truth lies. It lies in death. We believe in sex, in the economy, in culture, and in death. We believe that what it all comes down to in the end is death, that he screeches between his teeth as they clamp down on their prey, and we look at the centuries gone by from the height of this belief with indulgence and scorn, like everything looked at from a height. We cannot begrudge the past its errors. They were doubtless necessary. But now we have grown up. Now we believe only in what is powerful, reasonable, adult—and nothing is more childish than the light of a candle trembling in the darkness.

God. This poor thing, God, this crackling of light within light, this murmuring of silence to silence. This is what he talks to, Francis of Assisi, when he talks to the birds or to Clare, his little sister in carefreeness. He is in love. When you are in love, you talk to your love and to that alone. Everywhere, always. And what do you say to your love? You say that you love it, which is saying almost nothing—just the almost nothing of a smile, the stammering of a servant to a master who fulfills his wishes, who fulfills his wishes a thousand times over.

A few of his sayings have been packaged in a thin book, a real poor person's book. A few letters without beauty, prayers without grace, worn like a poor man's shirt that has been washed too many times, mended too often. A pastiche from the Bible. Here a bit of psalm, there another bit. It holds up well like that, it works well for the purpose: to pray, to speak to the emptiness so that the emptiness will cleanse your speech. I love you. That utterance, when it takes off toward God, is like a flaming arrow that flies deep into the night and goes out before reaching its target. I love you—that is his whole message, and that could never produce an original book, a writer's book. Love is nothing original. Love is not an author's invention.

He is with his love the way a child is with his ball in front of a wall. He throws his utterance, the ball of radiant utterance, the I-love-you rolled up on itself; he throws it against a wall that is separated from him by the distance of all the days he has left to live. Then he waits for the ball to bounce back. He throws thousands of balls. None of them ever comes back. He continues, always smiling: the game is its own reward, love is its own answer.

Well, yes, he does say a bit more. He says: I love you and I am sorry to love you so little, to love you so badly, to not know how to love you. The closer he gets to the light, the more he discovers himself as full of shadows. The more he loves, the more he recognizes himself as unworthy of loving. The fact is, there is no progress in love, no perfection that one might someday attain. No love is adult, mature, and reasonable. In relation to love there are only children—

there is only a spirit of childhood that is abandon, carefreeness, a spirit of letting go of spirit. Age adds up. Experience accumulates. Reason constructs. The spirit of childhood counts nothing, heaps up nothing, builds nothing. The spirit of childhood is always new, always starts afresh at the beginning of the world, with the first steps of love. The man of reason is an accumulated man, a heaped-up man, a constructed man. The man of childhood is the contrary of a man added on to himself: a man subtracted from himself, continually reborn in every birth of everything. He is an imbecile playing ball. Or a saint talking to his God. Or both at the same time.

There is something in the world that resists the world, and this thing is found neither in churches nor in cultures nor in the thoughts that people have about themselves, the deadly thoughts they have about themselves as serious, adult, and reasonable; and this thing is not a thing but God, and God cannot abide in anything without immediately shaking it up, without bringing it low. Huge God can abide only in the refrains of childhood, in the lost blood of the poor, or in the voice of plain, simple people. All of these hold God in the hollow of their open hands, a sparrow soaked like a piece of bread by the rain, a sparrow chilled to the bone, squawking, a chirping God who comes to eat from their naked hands.

God is what children know, not adults.

An adult has no time to waste feeding sparrows.

You Say You Love Me
and You Make Me
Feel Sad

THE THIRTEENTH CENTURY IS THE century of the crusades—foxes against wolves, Muslims against Christians. They are descendants of the same father buried under the Bible—Abraham. They fight each other with their teeth over his remains. Religion is what binds people together, and nothing is more religious than hatred: it brings men together on a large scale through the power of an idea or a name, whereas love frees them one by one through the weakness of a face or a voice. Francis of Assisi goes to Palestine to talk about a God whom crowds intimidate and churches irritate. He tells the soldiers the same thing as the sparrows. He does not talk in order to win them over: winning over is still gaining a victory, and the only victory he seeks is that of the feeble song, without the armor of iron or of language.

The light of Palestine caresses the waters of lakes and the names of prophets. It is no softer than that of Assisi. It is no truer than anywhere else. There is nothing in Palestine but an empty tomb. There is no Holy Land; the whole earth is holy, or else none of it is. He spends a few months in this light and then comes back to Europe, where he is needed. Thousands now follow in his footsteps, each thinking he possesses the truth of the way, confusing love with the fantasy he has about it. They want to play Francis's game but on the condition of changing the rules. For some these are too hard, for others they are not hard enough. On one side is hot-bloodedness, an anarchy of impulses. On the other is a stiffness of necks, an austerity of spirits. Therefore he has to recall the truth that something is not understood if it is understood only halfway. He has to say to some: you are seeking happiness in the tumult of your blood. Sometimes you find it, sometimes you lose it. But the joy I speak of to you is not at all like that. It is neither happy nor unhappy. It is carefree with regard to happiness and unhappiness, both. I do not ask you to seek within yourselves. I invite you to be like the naked earth, which is forgetful of itself; it gives the same welcome to the rain that beats upon it and to the sun that warms it. He has to say to the others: you are seeking perfection in the deserts of your spirit. But I do not ask you to be perfect. I ask you to be loving, which is not the same thing—which is so much not the same thing that it is quite the opposite. And then he has to say to all of them, brutally: when it comes down to it, I don't really know what I'm talking about when I talk about God. I speak without knowing. How could you, who pretend to hear and understand me, have greater knowledge above and beyond what I say than I do? You say you are becoming my companions, and you waste my heart. You say you love me and you make me feel sad. You make more noise than all the birds of the forest—and there is nothing on your lips that resembles a song. A singer burns in his voice. A lover exhausts himself in his love. Song is that burn, love is that weariness. I see you neither burned nor exhausted. You expect of love that it will fill and fulfill you. But love does not fill anything, not the hole you have in your head, not the abyss that you have in your heart. Love is an absence much more than a fullness. Love is a fullness of absence. This is, I grant you, an incomprehensible thing. But this thing that is impossible to understand is so very simple to live.

There comes a time when what a man has made of his life begins to close back in on him and suffocate him. You thought you were making your life, and now it comes about that your life is unmaking you. It is just such a misfortune that awaits Francis of Assisi on his return from Palestine. You had enough in your heart to burn the world. You did nothing more than invent one more religious order. And that is already a great deal. That great deal is not nothing. There are already, during your lifetime, libraries for Franciscan studies; there are theologians ruminating on the notion of poverty, turning the milk into ink, giving their parchments the care they refuse to people. You wanted there to be no more beggars' rags. There are now just a few more monks' habits.

Leaving. Leaving once more. Incessantly, endlessly leaving. Abraham left a first time, and this first time demanded everything of him, and this first time was impossible, and yet, all the same, it took place; and from this departing from everything, from this passion for the faraway, a son came to him, flesh of his flesh, joy of his joy. And then it happened that he was asked to leave once more, it happened that what he had done once, he had to do a second time, and this second time was just as impossible as the first and a thousand times harder, incomparably harder. It was nothing to leave his near and dear ones, to leave his language and his country. But then an insane God commanded him to cut himself off from his son—while living, to amputate himself from his life—a drunken God who was taking back His gift, was trampling on His word. For we are masters of nothing. What we create is immediately separated from us. Our creations are ignorant of us, our children are not our children. Moreover, we do not create anything. Nothing whatsoever. A man's days are to him what skins are to a snake. They shine for a time in the sun and then they come away. That is what awaits you, Francis of Provence, John of Assisi. You have to shed your skin a second time. And the first time will be of no help to you. The first time you left, and the world, after being amazed by this, called you back to tell you how charming it found your departure, how radiant it found your absence: those whom one cannot drown in the waters of scorn one suffocates by squeezing them in one's arms. Therefore you have to leave a second time, depart from your first departure. The world wants its sleep. The world is only sleep. The world wants the sleeping repetition of the world. But love wants awakening. Love is awakening reinvented each time, each time for the first time. The world conceives of no other end but death, that ecstasy of sleep, and it considers everything from the point of view of this end. First times—first steps, first smiles, first tears—are regarded by the world as necessarily leading to a second time that is easier than the first, less of a strain because more mechanical. And the second time will lead to a third time that is easier still, that is already sleepwalking, and thus, by a slow degradation, a necessary wearing down, the last time will be reached—the last yawn, the last languor of all. The child becomes the adult, and the adult goes to his death. There it is, the world's view. There is its miserable notion of life: a light trembling in its rising, for which the only possibility is to set. That is the view that you have to throw over. You have to leave a second time, and this departure has to be still newer than the first, more radically new, more lovingly new.

People grope blindly through their lives. Words are their white canes. These warn of obstacles, give the first shape to their blood. The word *route*, the dictionaries say, appeared in the thirteenth century, derived from the clayey matrix of the Latin word *rumpere*, "break violently," which became *rupta*, "road cleared in cutting a forest." This word is as though invented for Francis of Assisi, for a person for whom the route or road that opens into the world is shattered, broken. He is unfaithful to his family, unfaithful to everyone for the love of love, and describes with his curves a long straight line.

And now everything happens fast. A few years that pass like light, like water, like the wind. He writes the rule of life for his disciples. It is simple: rejoice the soul, be carefree about tomorrow, give your full attention to all living things. It is the happiness of not holding on to anything, the wonder of all presences. To make things even simpler for them, he tells this story. Do you want to know what joy is? Do you really want to know? Then listen. It's nighttime, it's raining, I'm hungry, I'm outside, I knock on the door of my house, I say it's me, and they don't let me in, I spend the night at the door of my house, in the rain, famished. There it is, that's joy. Let whoever can understand understand. Let whoever wants to hear hear. Joy is never again being home, being always outside, weakened by everything, hungry for everything, being everywhere in the out-of-doors of the world as in the belly of God.

Then he withdraws into the green solitude of the

trees, the gray solitude of the rocks. A disease touches his eyes, takes some of the strength from his eyes. Injured by the sun, he writes it a letter of thanks, a song of praise, his last salute to this life that he will have loved so much: "Praised be Thou, Lord, for our sister the earth, who sustains us and cares for us and gives us grass and colored flowers." This *Canticle of the Sun* has the obvious beauty of morning dew, of the first blush of dawn. There are two versions, with only a small difference between them. The second removes nothing that is in the first. After several weeks of silence, Francis of Assisi adds just one sentence, a dazzling sentence, light of language joined to silence: "Praised be Thou for our sister death."

"Praised be Thou for our sister death." He who writes this sentence, he who has the heart in him to pronounce it, has henceforth reached the farthest point of himself and the point closest to everything. Nothing separates him any longer from his love because his love is everywhere, even in that which is coming to break him.

"Praised be Thou for our sister death." He who murmurs this phrase has come to the end of the long labor of living, to the end of the separation that is put everywhere between life and our life. Three thicknesses of glass lie between the light and us, three thicknesses of time: From the past, the shadow of our parents, cast far forward over our life. From the present, the shadow of our acts and the image of us they secrete, fossilized, unbreakable. Francis of Assisi exhausted these two shadows, passed through these two sheets of glass with enough momentum not to wound himself on them. What is left is the ultimate test, the ultimate opacity that comes from the near future—the fear of dying, before which even the saints rear up like a horse refusing an obstacle at the last instant.

"Praised be Thou for our sister death." By casting his love far ahead of himself toward the shadow that is coming to take him, Francis of Assisi removes the last obstacle, like a wrestler defeating his adversary by taking him by the shoulders in order to embrace him.

"Praised be Thou for our sister death." So that has been said, that has been done. There is nothing left between life and his life, there is nothing left between himself and himself, there is no longer any past, any present, or any future, nothing left but God the Most Low, suddenly the Most High, suddenly spread everywhere like water.

The rest. Is it worthwhile to write the rest of what

apparently comes to an end on Saturday, October 3, 1226?

He slowly closes his eyes as under the charm of a profound thought, so profound that it makes him hold his breath.

A child. A child who breaks off his games without a visible reason and remains there, suddenly pale, immobile, mute, unable to do anything but smile.

Dirty Image, Holy Image

IN THE THIRTEENTH CENTURY, THERE are the merchants, the priests, and the soldiers. In the twentieth century, all that is left is the merchants. They are in their shops like priests in their churches. They are in their factories like soldiers in their barracks. They spread in the world through the power of their images. We find these on the walls, on the screens, in the newspapers. The image is their incense, the image is their sword. The thirteenth century spoke to the heart. It was not necessary for it to speak loudly to make itself heard. The songs of the Middle Ages hardly made more noise than snow falling on snow. The twentieth century speaks to the eye, and because sight is one of the most fickle senses, it has to shout, scream with violent lights, deafening colors, images that are appalling because they are so cheerful, images that are dirty because they are so clean, emptied of all shadow and all pain. Inconsolably cheerful images. This is because the twentieth century speaks in order to sell and therefore needs to flatter the eye—to flatter and blind it at the same time. Dazzle it. The thirteenth century has a lot less to sell. God has no price, He has only the commercial value of a snowflake falling on billions of other snowflakes.

The image was in the newspaper. You would have seen it when you read the article, not before then. We don't touch the world with the eyes but with the tongue. And what did the article say? It told of a thing of the end of the twentieth century, happening in a country like countries everywhere. Everywhere is money, everywhere is the world ruined by money. In this country, maybe a little more ruined than the others, the journalist describes the day of a family of beggars, their workday. They live in a poor part of an immense city, one of the world cities, cosmopoles, with twenty or thirty million inhabitants, one of those cities glutted with merchandise and souls, with blood, with gold, with mud. We see this family walking tens of kilometers, walking from a deprived neighborhood to a rich neighborhood, pushing a cart filled with a variety of things depending on the contents of the garbage cans. And here is the word that attracted your attention. Here is the word that made you see: the word *disposable*. This word, which at first designated the contents of the garbage cans, little by little has contaminated those who find their food in them. In this country, the article says, the journalists, the police, and even the sociologists finally have ended up referring to beggars as "disposables." And since a word never comes by itself, the article speaks about the operations of the police against these phantoms and their carts and of the benefits of a "social cleansing." The severity of the language, the terrifying severity of the language and of the law: indeed, what can one do with these "disposables" besides "cleanse" the world of their unworthy presence, so unfavorable to money, to the antiseptic cheerfulness of money?

You cut the photograph out of the newspaper. A nice family photo—the father and the mother in the foreground, surrounded by ten children with strangely radiant, open faces. Why did you keep this image? You weren't sure. To save it from disappearing with the transitoriness of the newspaper, to save it from the amnesia of the next day? To keep these smiling faces near you, the stubbornness of these presences

illuminated by garbage? It was after several days that
the thing happened. It was after several days that you
finally noticed the angel behind the group of children, a little masked by them, doubtless unperceived
by the photographer. It was necessary almost to close
your eyes, to create a very fine line of vision in order
to see him in the shadow of the children. He is too
busy, leaning as he is over a garbage can, rummaging
in it to see if by chance something more can be sal-
vaged, one more throw-away. And the other one—
you discovered him at the same time. At that moment
almost invisible, relegated to the background, to the
misty distances of the image, three steps to the rear,
nonchalant, following the trail of the children, the
cart, and the angel. You saw the other one, Tobias's
dog, with the joy in his gait, that crazy joy—the opposite of mercantile cheerfulness.

It was at that very moment that you understood
what you were in the presence of. It was in seeing the
joy of that mangy dog that you knew you were in the
presence of what is called a holy image.